"Wiman has found in *Every Riven Thing* his true voice, alternately edgy and relaxed, taut and unfettered. There's fear and grief, to be sure, but also consolation and humor." —KEVIN NANCE, *Poets & Writers*

"The work here is searingly honest and beautifully crafted, and it establishes Wiman in his most important public role: a gifted poet whose work cannot be ignored." —ELIZABETH LUND, *The Christian Science Monitor*

"This is haunting stuff—this is language turned and tuned to a pitch where it is both quiet scream and humble song." —BRIAN DOYLE, *The Christian Century*

"Few poets have been able to pull off contemplative/metaphysical poetry in the 20th and 21st centuries. Our detached sensibilities make that level of immersion feel overly forced. It can come off as both too submerged and too transcendent. We'd rather float. But Wiman makes a case for going old school. He dives right in to sentiment but swims up with hardly a drop of sentimentality. He asks for belief but never sounds fatuous. We are a god-hungry nation. Politicians know it, and it just might be time for poets to know it. Wiman, in this case, is ahead of the curve." —DEAN RADER, *The Rumpus*

T0057933

"Christian Wiman is fiercely dedicated to describing experiences for which there are no words—an ambition shared with many poets today. But few contemporary poets invite us to consider new ways of looking at those experiences as openly, intensely, and originally as he does." —MIKE PUICAN, *TriQuarterly*

"Wiman . . . writes with the gravity, awe, and humility of one who has been riven but lived to tell the tale, as well as ask the questions and pray the prayers that follow the experience of being broken . . . [His] use of violent imagery is reminiscent of Donne, while his reverence and musicality echo Hopkins, but the voice is his own." —*Image*Update

"Christian Wiman, the visionary editor of *Poetry* magazine, has written a book so urgent that the poems feel carved into the skin. Looming large over *Every Riven Thing* is Wiman's diagnosis with a rare form of cancer, but Wiman never slips into keening or self-dramatization; neither does he let the prospect of his death hurry his prosody. Instead, quite miraculously, he uses his considerable craft—measured, assured, but never belaboured—to slow what little time he may have left, and savour it in language as lush and full of pathos as one is likely to encounter in contemporary verse. He writes: 'To love is to feel your death / given to you like a sentence, / to meet the judge's eyes / as if there were a judge, / as if he had eyes / and love.' In doing so he reminds us that serious craft has an ethical, as well as aesthetic, quality to it." —MICHAEL LISTA, *National Post*

"I think you should go read this book, right now, and throw your-self into its brutal, beautiful simplicity . . . Wiman's poems speak of a survival, and a hope, that is neither bleak nor sentimental, but real and good and true. Praise to that, and to Wiman's rever-ence, which only has the power to assist our own." —ALLISON BACKOUS, *Comment*

"His is a world of acute insight into the human questions—of mortality, of God, of nature—rendered without proselytizing, without prognosis. He just observes, and still questions. He's as at home on the trains of the city as he is on the range of his native West Texas. He believes in God, yet leads us into the existential void, into the terror of the terminal soul. His illness sharpens his vision; his words are radiated. And yet, he's funny, using humor to disarm the darkness that lies within reach of his questions." —BRIAN HIEGGELKE, *Newcity*

"Christian Wiman . . . writes poems that are a study in torque, full of twisting force, words and lines pushing and pulling each other into forms of astonishing solidity and grace. His third collection, *Every Riven Thing*, is a beautiful and wrenching dialogue with death, decay, and the divine and is one of the best books of poems published last year." —JILL OWENS, PowellsBooks.Blog

DANIELLE CHAPMAN

CHRISTIAN WIMAN *Every Riven Thing*

Christian Wiman was born and raised in West Texas. He is the editor of *Poetry* and the author of two previous collections of poems, *The Long Home* (1998) and *Hard Night* (2005), and one collection of prose. He lives in Chicago.

every

riven

thing

CHRISTIAN WIMAN

FARRAR, STRAUS AND GIROUX

NEW YORK

every riven thing

Farrar, Straus and Giroux
18 West 18th Street, New York 10011

Published in 2010 by Farrar, Straus and Giroux
First paperback edition, 2011

The Library of Congress has cataloged
the hardcover edition as follows:
Wiman, Christian, 1966–
    Every riven thing / Christian Wiman.— 1st ed.
        p. cm.
    Poems.
    ISBN 978-0-374-15036-5
    I. Title.

PS3573.I47843E84 2010
811'.54—dc22

                                    2010012613

ISBN: 978-0-374-53306-9

Designed by Quemadura

www.fsgbooks.com

P1

for D.

CONTENTS

ĩ

ȶ ȶ ȶ

DUST DEVIL

Mystical hysterical amalgam of earth and wind
and mind

over and of
the much-loved

dust you go
through a field I know

by broken heart
for I have learned this art

of flourishing
vanishing

wherein to live
is to move

cohesion
illusion

wild untouchable toy
called by a boy

God's top
in a time when time stopped

No remembering now
when the apple sapling was blown
almost out of the ground.
No telling how,
with all the other trees around,
it alone was struck.
It must have been luck,
he thought for years, so close
to the house it grew.
It must have been night.
Change is a thing one sleeps through
when young, and he was young.
If there was a weakness in the earth,
a give he went down on his knees
to find and feel the limits of,
there is no longer.
If there was one random blow from above
the way he's come to know
from years in this place,

the roots were stronger.

Whatever the case,

he has watched this tree survive

wind ripping at his roof for nights

on end, heats and blights

that left little else alive.

No remembering now . . .

A day's changes mean all to him

and all days come down

to one clear pane

through which he sees

among all the other trees

this leaning, clenched, unyielding one

that seems cast

in the form of a blast

that would have killed it,

as if something at the heart of things,

and with the heart of things,

had willed it.

FIVE HOUSES DOWN

I loved his ten demented chickens
and the hell-eyed dog, the mailbox
shaped like a huge green gun.
I loved the eyesore opulence
of his five partial cars, the wonder-cluttered porch
with its oilspill plumage, tools
cauled in oil, the dark
clockwork of disassembled engines
christened Sweet Baby and benedicted Old Bitch;
and down the steps into the yard the explosion
of mismatched parts and black scraps
amid which, like a bad sapper cloaked
in luck, he would look up stunned,
patting the gut that slopped out of his undershirt
and saying, *Son,*
you lookin' to make some scratch?
All afternoon we'd pile the flatbed high
with stacks of Exxon floormats
mysteriously stenciled with his name,

rain-rotted sheetrock or miles
of misfitted pipes, coil after coil
of rusted fencewire that stained for days
every crease of me, rollicking it all
to the dump where, while he called
every ragman and ravened junkdog by name,
he catpicked the avalanche of trash
and fished some always fixable thing
up from the depths. His endless aimless work
was not work, my father said.
His barklike earthquake curses
were not curses, for he could *goddamn*
a slipped wrench and *shitfuck* a stuck latch,
but one bad word from me
made his whole being
twang like a nail mis-struck. *Ain't no call for that,*
Son, no call at all. Slipknot, whatknot,
knot from which no man escapes—
prestoed back to plain old rope;
whipsnake, blacksnake, deep in the wormdirt
worms like the clutch of mud:
I wanted to live forever
five houses down
in the womanless rooms a woman
sometimes seemed to move through, leaving him

twisting a hand-stitched dishtowel
or idly wiping the volcanic dust.
It was heaven to me:
beans and weenies from paper plates,
black-fingered tinkerings on the back stoop
as the sun set, on an upturned fruitcrate
a little jamjar of rye like ancient light,
from which, once, I took a single, secret sip,
my eyes tearing and my throat on fire.

To grasp at the mercury minnows are
or were

in childhood's kingdom
lord of boredom

is to see
through an intimate, ultimate clarity

that galaxy shatter
and like a mind of matter

resolve itself star by slow star.
To grasp at the mercury minnows are ...

Brachest, she called it, gentling grease
over blanching yolks with an expertise
honed from three decades of dawns
at the Longhorn Diner in Loraine,
where even the oldest in the old men's booth
swore as if it were scripture truth
they'd never had a breakfast better,
rapping a glass sharply to get her
attention when it went sorrowing
so far into some simple thing—
the jangly door or a crusted pan,
the wall clock's black, hitchy hands—
that she would startle, blink, then grin
as if discovering them all again.
Who remembers now when one died
the space that he had occupied
went unfilled for a day, then two, three,
until she unceremoniously
plunked plates down in the wrong places

and stared their wronged faces
back to banter she could hardly follow.
Unmarried, childless, homely, "slow,"
she knew coffee cut with chamomile
kept the grocer Paul's ulcer cool,
yarrow in gravy eased the islands
of lesions in Larry Borwick's hands,
and when some nightlong nameless urgency
sent him seeking human company
Brother Tom needed hash browns with cheese.
She knew to nod at the litany of cities
the big-rig long-haulers bragged her past,
to laugh when the hunters asked
if she'd pray for them or for the quail
they went laughing off to kill,
and then—envisioning one
rising so fast it seemed the sun
tugged at it—to do exactly that.
Who remembers where they all sat:
crook-backed builders, drought-faced farmers,
VF'ers muttering through their wars,
night-shift roughnecks so caked in black
it seemed they made their way back
every morning from the dead.
Who remembers one word they said?

The Longhorn Diner's long torn down,
the gin and feedlots gone, the town
itself now nothing but a name
at which some bored boy has taken aim,
every letter light-pierced and partial.
Sister, Aunt Sissy, Bera Thrailkill,
I picture you one dime-bright dawn
grown even brighter now for being gone
bustling amid the formica and chrome
of that small house we both called home
during the spring that was your last.
All stories stop: once more you're lost
in something I can merely see:
steam spiriting out of black coffee,
the scorched pores of toast, a bowl
of apple butter like edible soil,
bald cloth, knifelight, the lip of a glass,
my plate's gleaming, teeming emptiness.

ALL GOOD CONDUCTORS

I.

O the screech and heat and hate
we have for each day's commute,

the long wait at the last stop
before we go screaming

underground, while the pigeons
court and shit and rut

insolently on the tracks
because this train is always late,

always aimed at only us,
who when it comes with its

blunt snout, its thousand mouths,
cram and curse and contort

into one creature, all claws and eyes,
tunneling, tunneling, tunneling

toward money.

2.

Sometimes a beauty
cools through the doors at Grand,

glides all the untouchable
angles and planes

of herself
to stand among us

like a little skyscraper,
so sheer, so spare,

gazes going all over her
in a craving wincing way

like sun on glass.

3.

There is a dreamer
all good conductors

know to look for
when the last stop is made

and the train is ticking cool,
some lover, loner, or fool

who has lived so hard
he jerks awake

in the graveyard,
where he sees

coming down the aisle
a beam of light

whose end he is,
and what he thinks are chains

becoming keys.

Flip-flops, leash-clinks,
spit on the concrete
like a light slap:
our dawn goon
ambles past, flexing
his pit bull. And soft,
and soon, a low burn
lights the flight path
from O'Hare,
slowly the sky
a roaring flue
to heaven
slowly shut.
Here's a curse
for a car door
stuck for the umpteenth
time, here a rake
for next door's nut
to claw and claw

at nothing. My nature
is to make
of the speedbump
scraping the speeder's
undercarriage,
and the *om*
of traffic, and somewhere
the helicopter
hovering over
snarls—a kind
of clockwork
from which all things
seek release,
but it takes
particular clicks
to pique my poodle's
interest, naming
with her nose's
particular quiver
the unseeable
unsayable
squirrel. Good girl.

THE MOLE

After love
discovers it,
the little burn
or birthmark
in an odd spot
he can neither see
nor reach; after
the internist's
downturned mouth,
specialists leaning
over him like
diviners, machines
reading his billion
cells; after
the onslaught
of insight, cures
crawling through him
like infestations,
so many surgeries

a wrong move
leaves him leaking
like overripe fruit;
after the mountain
aster and ice
wine, Michigan
football, *Canes*
Venatici and
the Four North
Fracture Zone
shrink to a room
where voices grow
hushed as if
at some holy
place, and even
in the kindest
eye there lurks
the eternity
to which he's been
commended; after
speech, touch,
even the instinct
to eat are gone,
and he has become
nothing but
a collection of quiet

tics and twitches
as if something
wanted out
of his riddled
bones, the carious
maze of his brain;
as the last day
glaciers into his room,
glass and chrome
so infinites-
imally facet-
ed it seems
he lives inside
a diamond, he breaks
into a wide
smile, as if joy
were the animal
in him, blind,
scrabbling, earth-
covered creature
tunneling ·
up from God
knows where to stand
upright, feasting
on distances, gazing
dead into the sun.

DARKCHARMS

In the waiting room, alive together, alone together,
bright hives humming inside of us, in spite of us ...

■

Radiated, palliated, sheened gray like infected meat,
he takes my hand, gratified, mystified, as if we'd met on the moon.

■

Needle of knowledge, needle of nothingness,
grinding through my spine to sip at the marrow of me.

■

To be so touched, so known, so beloved of nothing:
a kind of chewed-tinfoil shiver of the soul.

■

Animate iron, black junk, seared feelerless, up crawls
my cockroach hope, lone survivor of the fire I am.

■

In the world the world's unchanged to all but you:
iodine dawns, abyss of birdsong, a friend's laughter lashes
    invisible whips.

■

How are *you*? Pity soaks the moment like wet bread.
Do I spit it out, or must I gum this unguent down?

■

Philosophy of treatment regimens, scripture of obituaries:
heretic, lunatic, I touch my tumor like a charm.

■

Prevarications, extenuations, tomorrow's tease of being:
we are what we are only in our last bastions.

■

And past that?
Now, near me, not me, a girl, shameless, veinless, screams.

God goes, belonging to every riven thing he's made
sing his being simply by being
the thing it is:
stone and tree and sky,
man who sees and sings and wonders why

God goes. Belonging, to every riven thing he's made,
means a storm of peace.
Think of the atoms inside the stone.
Think of the man who sits alone
trying to will himself into a stillness where

God goes belonging. To every riven thing he's made
there is given one shade
shaped exactly to the thing itself:
under the tree a darker tree;
under the man the only man to see

God goes belonging to every riven thing. He's made
the things that bring him near,

made the mind that makes him go.
A part of what man knows,
apart from what man knows,

God goes belonging to every riven thing he's made.

God let me give you now this mind of dying
fevering me back
into consciousness of all I lack
and of that consciousness becoming proud:

> *There are keener griefs than God.*
> *They come quietly, and in plain daylight,*
> *leaving us with nothing, and the means to feel it.*

My God my grief forgive my grief tamed in language
to a fear that I can bear.
Make of my anguish
more than I can make. Lord, hear my prayer.

ONE TIME

1. Canyon de Chelly, Arizona

Then I looked down into the lovely cut
of a missing river, something under
dusk's upflooding shadows
claiming for itself a clarity
of which my eyes were not yet capable:
fissures could be footpaths, ancient homes
random erosions; pictographs depicting fealties
of who knows what hearts, to who knows what gods.
To believe is to believe you have been torn
from the abyss, yet stand waveringly on its rim.
I come back to the world. I come back
to the world and would speak of it plainly,
with only so much artifice as words
themselves require, only so much distance
as my own eyes impose
on the slickrock whorls of the real
canyon, the yucca's stricken

clench, and, on the other side,
the dozen buzzards swirled and buoyed
above some terrible intangible fire
that must scald the very heart
of matter to cast up such avid ash.

2. 2047 *Grace Street*

But the world is more often refuge
than evidence, comfort and covert
for the flinching will, rather than the sharp
particulate instants through which God's being burns
into ours. I say God and mean more
than the bright abyss that opens in that word.
I say world and mean less
than the abstract oblivion of atoms
out of which every intact thing emerges,
into which every intact thing finally goes.
I do not know how to come closer to God
except by standing where a world is ending
for one man. It is still dark,
and for an hour I have listened
to the breathing of the woman I love beyond
my ability to love. Praise to the pain
scalding us toward each other, the grief

beyond which, please God, she will live
and thrive. And praise to the light that is not
yet, the dawn in which one bird believes,
crying not as if there had been no night
but as if there were no night in which it had not been.

FROM A WINDOW

Incurable and unbelieving
in any truth but the truth of grieving,

I saw a tree inside a tree
rise kaleidoscopically

as if the leaves had livelier ghosts.
I pressed my face as close

to the pane as I could get
to watch that fitful, fluent spirit

that seemed a single being undefined
or countless beings of one mind

haul its strange cohesion
beyond the limits of my vision

over the house heavenwards.
Of course I knew those leaves were birds.

Of course that old tree stood
exactly as it had and would

(but why should it seem fuller now?)
and though a man's mind might endow

even a tree with some excess
of life to which a man seems witness,

that life is not the life of men.
And that is where the joy came in.

They were good times, the end times
(as the preacher called them)
when there was no remoteness that was not wired,
it was possible to live entirely inside,
and every ozone sundown burned a braver creation.

That was the summer when the year was summer.
Smokestacks curlicued their smog
in almost animal shapes,
and the whole nation came together
to watch the two-headed infant speak its first word
on TV.

We were at the edge: I remember music
comprised entirely of surgical sounds;
a daylong documentary
in which a glacier made a lace of ice so fine
the contemplation of that loss
isolated and annihilated time
like a mystic discipline.

True, there were wars,
and, true, in some sense they were ours.
But rage was ... all the rage—
a dinner-party flinch and grimace
by which the like-minded linked (and liked) their minds.

It made little sense to love, but love we did,
flinging ourselves out of ourselves like a river
striking rock
—suspended upended bits of light
grown gloriously plural—
before the tug and the rush and the roar of us onward.

Of course there were things we had to let go.
The fish in the harbor, kaleidoscopic even at night,
floated like rotting rainbows as they died.

Of course there were those whom pills could no longer lift,
with their novels and their pillows,
as if a mildest light were eating them.

And the sandwich boards selling salvation.
And the engine-eyed atheists screaming reason.

Even the preacher, like a private winter, whitened, and quietened,
then one Sunday instead of speaking

burned his sermon
so that, he whispered over the ashes after,
there might be finally one fire our eyes would see.

And indeed that day did feel different.
It seemed there was not one of us
not one of us.
Peace rumored through our screens like a breeze.
The sun itself had the shy, pain-shined air of a survivor.
Even the ocean, it was said, was open.

That evening when the sky like a brandied mind
seemed to dream us at our windows
we met each other's eyes and shook our heads
as if we couldn't believe
what we had been given, how beautiful it had been,
and indeed still was,
slurring such last extravagant streaks of light
over the endless city.

It should be so pointedly, painfully human
it hints of machine, like a naked anorexic.
It should, while evoking eternity, cry time,
like a priest at meat.

Let our public buildings proclaim their separateness.
Let our flag be fearsome.
Let our money mean even more to us.

And do not forget:
a west vast as unconsciousness,
arteries of oil, oceans warm as urine.

Consider icicle skyscrapers,
parthenogenetic subdivisions,
factory farms in which a billion breasts with beaks
inflate to fill their cages,
satellites so fine they're triggered by sighs . . .

We vacuumed fat. We erected glitter.
We invented memory and made of it
a Web, a Predator, an Avatar.

We gave our name to a new disease.
We creatured nature with our cries.

The wind is one force
the houses break.

It howls around the doors
before the people wake

to news of wars
fought for their sake

on arid, alien shores.
Hard blasts rake

power boats at the wharves
along the lake,

the little specialty stores
bang and shake

—until, as if with remorse
for some mistake

or there were one force
force could slake—

it all goes soft as snores,
murmurs, some vague ache,

as if dreams were a course
a storm might take,

a people's hearts its source,
their bones its wake.

What grew there grew in tangled
ways, minor thrivings of thorntrees, shocked
cacti, tumbleweeds maddening
past in the cages of themselves, everywhere a sense of
sharpness and thwartedness, he the last
twisted try of it all. Light meant
work. He honed
a little horizon of iron and dawn,
bowed all day over acres of adamant
flint as if he were sowing sparks. He found
shells brittling back toward their sea,
leaves and twigs more sun
than themselves, and a thousand other fragments
eternity was tugging at,
and wrought it all into a tenuous, tenacious form
as if he were founding ruins—
a man who himself seemed half born,
half hewn, his skin mapped
with damage, sweat slicking the juts and
cliffs of flesh, eyes so like the sky

he seemed at once all-seeing and all skull.
What did he ask of us, who did not once
acknowledge us, came not once among us,
though we woke to footprints
scalding our lawns, a leprosy
of emptiness gone through all our goods?
What covenant did he keep or rage
to break, his shadow flickering
ceaselessly beside him and the distance stricken
with waves as if some bell of being itself
had sounded? He struck
rock and the rootless dust down to a clay that gave
and gave until he was altogether
underground, smoldering
into sleep, worms of dreams
working under his brow. He climbed
to the only rise there was, the cleft
of rock where the huge beehive hung
like nature's brain, suffering himself
to taste its sweetness. He wrung
from time a time to vanish
back into the sheer
shells and the strict mesquites, the heat-cracked
creekbed and the needless weeds, leaving us
to sift the glorious
ash of his existence, like a burned sermon.

How to say this—
my silences were not always mine:
scrabbled hole and the black beyond;
vaporous pond
as if water wanted out of itself;
tip of the sycamore's weird bare reach:
some latency in things leading not so much to speech
as to a halting, haunted art
wherein to master was to miss—
how to say this, how to say this . . .

My father was a boatbuilder.
Prow of a man, his world a sea to cleave.
I learned a dangerous patience,
to navigate night, live on nothing, leave.
And my mother, her furious smallness,
her way of saying her blade, the oil and onion's hiss:
from her I learned what lies beneath.

Mystic, Istanbul, Jakarta, Dar es Salaam—
what was I meant to keep?
If the distances to which I've been given
suggest some wantless heaven
of the mind, what in me still traces
the creekbed creases
in the rough skin of the palm
of one so long asleep?

If I say I loved the seagull
tethered to its cry, the cypress's imprisoned winds,
speak to the brink of my hands
a moss-covered rock
soft and knobby as a kitten's skull.
If I say I loved.

Boston, Lisbon, Cardiff, Asunción:
what name is not a horizon?
Somewhere it is evening,
light grown mild and pliable,
wielded by wave and rock,
in the shore's trees torn apart . . .

Do you remember the rude nudists?

Lazing easy in girth and tongue,
wet slops and smacks of flesh as they buttered every crevice.

Sungrunts. Blubberpalaver.

We were always hiking some hill toward some beauty some
    human meanness ruined.
We were always waiting too long to let ourselves be seen.

It was an ocean's gesticulations, articulate elephant seals,
    grounded clouds grown all one mouth.

What could we do but laugh,
casting clothes aside as if the air were ice and water a warm bed,
goose-stepping goose-pimpled past their appeased surprise into
    the waves.

What could we do?

We could—we did—love
take a long look
at each other
    and creep quietly away.

The bumps and hush, the little furtive rustlings
that half-woke me last night wake me now

                                   as the goateed cheeseman
tells me his son's tongue is pierced
        (gleams, pungencies)
slicing with strong displeasure Sardinian Gold.

And that initial chill before I knew going again like a dew
through me as I walk down the dogrun

                             where the birdlady
wielding with bad English and old bread
pigeons like a single sinuous body
stretches out her arms and, amid descending wings
and low moans, stands completely still:

drunk kids crawling into the unlit alcove
to smoke and fuck in the small hours.

                             Tenuous the hold
she has on them, furious the need she knows

will bring them always eventually within her reach,
a fire of eyes and appetite whipping around her knees
settling fluttering along each outstretched arm
as if to lift her out of this life.

I could almost hear my heart beat . . .

Palm trees and eucalyptus, the salt breeze and palpable clouds,
a siren somewhere dying on the mild air
as I head up my street
                              where the runner pauses,
pearled as if she's spent the night outside,
fine dunes in her legs as she leans
to read the headlines.

1. Dipped into Frenzy

Dipped into frenzy
                                  like a tonged lobster
he squeaked a bit
then stopped

Overnight
                      his hair went white

Clean-suited
in a rocking chair
that never rocked
                              with a smile
that either included or excluded
utterly

he was every kind of crying
but the kind that you can see

2. *Like a Dog Existence Is*

Lame, bees in his brain, two teeth shy
of total gum
       he bites the air

Like a dog existence is
persistent in him:
         he bites the air

        ■

So gifted in misery, such disciplined self-pity,
and now, to make his helplessness a hell
for others, to make them loathe themselves
for loathing him:
        his masterwork.

        ■

When there is nothing left to curse
you can curse nothing
but when there is nothing left to love
the heart eats inward and inward its own need
for release . . .

■

Chained to his fate, he spits
memory, wastes
to a gaze, and dies
with still-unexpended hatred in his eyes
like a dog.

3. *Not Altogether Gone*

Not altogether gone
his antic frantic penny-ante-Ahab stabs of madness

honeybunching the stewardess, teasing a little pile
of eyebrows on his tray-table like impossible pixie sticks

swiveling to give the loud grout rep what for
two cloudminded miles over Iowa

then subsiding spastically back
into his particular contortion of quiet

frieze-faced, mouth an unhappened howl, one arm
half-raised half-childlike as if to ask or answer . . .

before he's seized again with a sharp impersonal turbulence
like angry laundry

4. *Fuck Dominoes*

"I'll follow your toenails
into any hell that you propose
so deeply do they mean your feet
so purely is their pink my soul's

Teach me to polka my walker
to hum dementia's tune
and I'll don diapers with a kinky gleam
slurp stewed prunes with oyster joy

O my pretties cantankered into twisty things
my lonesome irksome debutantes of death
I'll be the girling dervish of Royal Estates
your bug-eyed undruggable, your ear-hair boy"

5. American Cheese

To live amid the jackal looks of unlove,
all the relatives circling eerily warily the scent
of their own blood.
                              Some want money, some seek
only peace, but to you the teeth gleam with the same
obscene rapacity.
                        So you rouse yourself
of an afternoon, not leaving your lair
so much as carrying it with you, that moist, almost visible
nimbus of pain, urine, cold coffee, and cable news
crackling occasionally through the stale cloud of it all—

for an outing! a bit of nature, a refreshing stagger
through the fluorescent plains of Wal-Mart:

demons inked on arms, nicotine tans, hoosegow gazes,
chemical grins, galactic buttocks, some terrycloth termagant

shrilling at her overblooded underminded whelp
Slim! That boy. Goddammit Slim. Slim!

Welcome to the hell of having everything:
one repentant politician on sixty screens,
van-sized vats of crabgrass toxin,
a solid quarter mile of disposable diapers:
all our impossibles pluraled.

Would Daddy like some rectal gel?
Would Daddy like some single-use oral swabs?
Would Daddy like some Clonezapam Hydrocodone Lyrica
    Trazodone Cymbalta Wellbutrin Lipitor Vesicare?

Yes, Daddy would.

And Daddy would like to go home, too,
you say without saying a word, minding
your invisible balance beam through the unfuturistic
suck-sound of the doors into the incinerator summer
even locusts have brains enough
to stay out of—
                    everywhere abandoned
carts, triceratops-looking trucks, mother upon mother
with a hungry aboriginal howl

coming not quite from her—
                              while beside you
some dropsical shambles of humanity
who could be your grandson or your grandfather
slimes his sluglike fingers into your own
to press a little *God Is Love* medallion still sticky
from its Cracker Jack box—

though, come to think of it, you'd never find such a thing there,
would you?

6. *As in a Freak Nook*

As in a freak nook of cliff
it would take a lonely soul to descend and see
a kinked tree grows a moment
still as the rock in which it's rooted—
I saw through his wildtime the childtime smile.

7. Now, When There Is No Now to Burn

Now, when there is no now to burn,
and those who, despite you, loved you, turn
back to their lives and the fact of your absence
the strangeness is how little strangeness there is
in the blank day, the meaningless depletion, the grief.
It was always all aftermath, your life.

A good landscape for grief
has no hill higher than a furrow,
a few gouty cacti,
perhaps a withered tree or two
if only to remind you
of what's missing.
Depression is a wet word, with ripe vines,
claustrophobic moss, endless dripping
instants which here have no more
purchase on the earth
than a tear from an armadillo's eye.
It is a relief, really, to be so scoured
of one's own maudlin drama, or lack of drama,
to move through what feels
at once like a fate and utter absence
of that, as if walking all a long day a life
of something you couldn't say
you come to a country
funeral at which you have no reason

to be: faceless names, unmothering
bosoms, past-lacquered suits,
eyes too rapt and intent to weep.
We are gathered here to mark one man
passing. He is your father
and your son, my mother and my self.
Let us sing this city of instants
come back to be a part of us.
Let us carry through the tiny eternities
of our minds this one hole
in time, beside which a boy
who has our hands is rearranging his face
as if it were clay, and a moment
opens and opens in the end
of days like a rose
on which a bee in all its hirsute specificity
has landed, its feelers feeling
everything as it crawls slowly inside,
and never comes out.

JOUISSANCE

All night I lay twisting
basting in my anxiety
trying to remember
how to pronounce the word never
in my life and perhaps least
now have I had occasion to use
though it is from this distance
hardly difficult for instance
my father's wasp-nested senescence
my mother's metallic cheer
my brother's primordial poverty
my sister's tired drug-tongued drawl
each might conceivably speak
what I in my anxiety
could not say if he or she
or we I mean all of us were
standing for instance in a Parisian
street a toxic prospect
neutralized somehow by the smell

of Frito pie from the *boulangerie*
and the not-quite-cold-enough-to-snow
night snowing harmlessly into
silence so alien the only
sound in the moment
before one of us for all of us
speaks is the little *click click* of nails
and teeth as over the pavingstones
a ridiculous red-jacketed
poodle leaps twisting biting
snowflakes like miracle toys

Madden me back to an afternoon
I carry in me
not like a wound
but like a will against a wound

Give me again enough man
to be the child
choosing my own annihilations

To make of this severed limb
a wand to conjure
a weapon to shatter
dark matter of the dirt daubers' nests
galaxies of glass

Whacking glints
bash-dancing on the cellar's fire
I am the sound the sun would make
if the sun could make a sound

and the gasp of rot
stabbed from the compost's lumpen living death
is me

O my life my war in a jar
I shake you and shake you
and may the best ant win

For I am come a whirlwind of wasted things
and I will ride this tantrum back to God

until my fixed self, my fluorescent self
my grief-nibbling, unbewildered, wall-to-wall self
withers in me like a salted slug

HAMMER IS THE PRAYER

There is no consolation in the thought of God,
he said, slamming another nail

in another house another havoc had half-taken.
Grace is not consciousness, nor is it beyond.

To hell with remembrance, to hell with heaven,
hammer is the prayer of the poor and the dying.

And as wind in some lordless random comes to rest,
and all the disquieted dust within,

peace came to the hinterlands of our minds,
too remote to know, but peace nonetheless.

WHEN THE TIME'S TOXINS

When the time's toxins
have seeped into every cell

and like a salted plot
from which all rain, all green, are gone

I and life are leached
of meaning

somehow a seed
of belief

sprouts the instant
I acknowledge it:

little weedy hardy would-be
greenness

tugged upward
by light

while deep within
roots like talons

are taking hold again
of this our only earth.

As through a long-abandoned half-standing house
only someone lost could find,

which, with its paneless windows and sagging crossbeams,
its hundred crevices in which a hundred creatures hoard and nest,

seems both ghost of the life that happened there
and living spirit of this wasted place,

wind seeks and sings every wound in the wood
that is open enough to receive it,

shatter me God into my thousand sounds . . .

There is a lake from which no sun returns.
Brown, glintless, it lies in the land like the land.
A man might be forgiven for thinking he
might walk that water like any acre's dirt,
might stride the man-made dam like a god in mind.

■

If it is grief that brings him here, it is
a grief in which the land participates,
a dry grief, a grief of heat, in which the trees'
contortions tighten and the cacti crouch.
He stares and stares at the unchanging lake.

■

Neither the shy possum nor rare mule deer,
nor horned toad with its tough embattled back,
nor tenuously existing crane, nor billion years
of armadillo clenched around one heart:
if creatures come they come to sip the dark.

■

Can this still be a source? Can a stranger
still claim to taste what the whole town denies,
that taint of earth in the purest glass, some ghost
of dust that brings almost a further thirst?
It is a taste to which one grows accustomed.

■

If a mountain moved, if the whirlwind knew
his name, if there arose around him a city
of jasper, still, this leaching heat would be
his dream, his chance at home, this shrunken lake
where all his jigsawed creekbeds pour their nothings.

■

Over the lake, out of the mind, a small whine
finds a form, a time, his father at the wheel.
He'll rock the bow, he'll tickle catastrophe,
but not now, not here, just this trim craft
skimming the water, lighter than water, and the small whine.

■

Kneeling in mud, shirted because he's burned,
already badly burned, humming some nothing,
lost in the long atomic pause of childhood,
head bowed, cheeks bright, finger-streaked with black
as if the dark he worked on worked on him . . .

■

What god more dead than the god of childhood? What child
more gone than the wandering one, the heedless one,
whom parents drown to keep their children near?
He has no name, no home, no certain birth,
is never found because he never was.

．

He stares and stares at the unchanging lake,
which—past the shallows, where to his truant eyes
the best schools used to rise—changes: soft pocks,
small sparks, as of some clear aboriginal rain
so light, so lost, that light is all it is.

．

Deep in the beargrass and the broomweed, deep
in time, two teens whom time has torn apart
have spread a blanket, borne their bodies toward
the little oblivion they call, rightly, love,
and made of the air an unguent made of them.

．

She who in her last days loved too well to lose
a single weed to namelessness, in creosote,
blue grama, goatsbeard that is not thriving, is,
amid the cattails' brittle whisper whispers
O Law', Honey, ain't this a praiseful thing.

．

A shadow on the water soft as thought
slows, wavers gently, as if some shadowy life
with which it might be one, be none, beckoned,
before the life to which it's tethered tugs
and the high bird that knows to keep on going goes.

■

What fights so hard to stay unknown, unnamed?
Before the eyes fix inward and the scales are scraped off;
before the larval innards—the migrained reds,
abysmal blacks—glop back into the brown water,
there is this line pulled taut. This grip. This glee.

■

Say a child, a man, any creature quick with being
broke this sullen plane, it would seem the ground
grew fluent as he moved, a slow undulance
of earth in which he floated, vanished, rose, was—
if some distant someone were to see it.

■

There comes a time when time is not enough:
a hand takes hold or a hand lets go; cells swarm,
cease; high and cryless a white bird blazes beyond
itself, to be itself, burning unconsumed.
There comes a time when it is time to be

■

alive by a lake where the sun dies and dies.
Brown, glintless, it lies in the land and in the mind.
A man might be forgiven for loving dust,
dead weeds and a cracked, receding shore,
a sky so empty that it has no end.

Groans going all the way up a young tree
half-cracked and caught in the crook of another

pause. All around the hill-ringed, heavened pond
leaves shush themselves like an audience.

A cellular stillness, as of some huge attention
bearing down. May I hold your hand?

A clutch of mayflies banqueting on oblivion
writhes above the water like visible light.

I SING INSOMNIA

I sing insomnia
         to the minor devils
prowling alleys
      of my mind

loneliness's lipsticked leer
               fear
no fix can case
        envy sipping bile

I make a lullaby
        to make myself
into a sleeper
       of the faith

awake
    my little while
alive
    without a why

Then I slept into a terror world
where things gave back my gaze:
baffled grass, a fury tree, dirt
disinterring grief by means of me.

I suffered a river's memories,
rock's archaic ache, all the soft
improvisations of the brain-shaped,
breeze-shaped clouds.

I was rifled, pilfered, praised, used.
I was lifted up into the rain's mania,
laid cadaverously down amid the avid seeps
and intuitive roots, a little slime

of life crawling through me
like an inchoate incarnate thought
beyond God, beyond art, beyond all idea
of beyond. Then I woke with a start.

LORD IS NOT A WORD

Lord is not a word.
Song is not a salve.
Suffer the child, who lived
on sunlight and solitude.
Savor the man, craving
earth like an aftertaste.
To discover in one's hand
two local stones the size
of a dead man's eyes
saves no one, but to fling them
with a grace you did not know
you knew, to bring them
skimming homing
over blue, is to discover
the river from which they came.
Mild merciful amnesia
through which I've moved
as through a blue atmosphere
of almost and was,

how is it now,
like ruins unearthed by ruin,
my childhood should rise?
Lord, suffer me to sing
these wounds by which I am made
and marred, savor this creature
whose aloneness you ease and are.

So much a poet he despises poetry
wary weary of the tempest in him
his soul's dainties

                as in a gruff wind
between buildings downtown
a sculpted modern
woman

       keeps her hands tight
to her thighs
to keep her skirt

            from flying up!

Given a god more playful
more sayful
           less prone
to unreachable peaks
and silence at the heart
of stone

I might have plundered
thunder
           from a tick's back

I might have swigged
existence
           from a tulip's bell

and given all hell
to a god who given time

knew goddamn well
what to do with it:

make, and proliferate,
and vanish
        when you are through with it

LORD OF HAVING

Lord of having
hell at hand
Lord of losing
what I have
this heaven now

may I move
in time
like a cloud
in sky
my torn form
the wind's
one sign

may my suffering be
speechless
clarity
as of water
in some reach

of rock
it would take
work
to ascend
and see

and may my hands
my eyes
the very nub
of my tongue
be scrubbed
out of this hour
if I should utter
the dirty word
eternity

IT IS GOOD TO SIT EVEN A ROTTING BODY

for W. S. Di Piero

It is good to sit even a rotting body
in sunlight uncompromised
by God, or lack of God,

to see the bee beyond
all the plundered flowers
air-stagger toward you

and like a delicate helicopter
hover above your knee
until it finds you to be

not sweet but at least
not flinching, its hair-legs
on the hair of your leg

silvering
a coolness through you
like a soul of nerve.

Dawn is a dog's yawn, space
in bed where a body should be,
a nectared yard, night surviving
in wires through which what voices,
what needs already move—and the mind
nibbling, nibbling at Nothingness
like a mouse at cheese:

Spring!

∎

Sometimes one has the sense
that to say the name
God is a great betrayal,
but whether one is betraying
God, language, or one's self
is harder to say.

∎

Gone for the day, she is the day
opening in and around me
like flowers she planted in our yard.
Christ. Not flowers.
Gone for the day, she is the day
razoring in with the Serbian roofers,
and ten o'clock tapped exactly
by the one bad wheel of the tortilla cart,
and the newborn's noonday anguish
eased. And the *om* the mind
makes of traffic and the bite
of reality that brings it back.
And the late afternoon afterlight
in which a much-loved dog lies
like a piece of precocious darkness
lifting his ears at threats, treats, comings, goings . . .

■

To love is to feel your death
given to you like a sentence,
to meet the judge's eyes
as if there were a judge,
as if he had eyes,
and love.

ACKNOWLEDGMENTS

Grateful acknowledgment is made to the editors of the following publications, where the poems in this book, sometimes in different form, first appeared: *The American Scholar, The Atlantic Monthly, CellPoems, The Christian Century, Design Observer, First Things, Harvard Divinity Bulletin, Image, The New Criterion, The New England Review, The New Ohio Review, The New Republic, The New Yorker, Orion, Poetry Daily, Poetry International, Poetry Northwest, Quirk,* and *Slate.*

I am also very grateful to Ilya Kaminsky for his insight, honesty, and example.

Printed in the USA
CPSIA information can be obtained
at www.ICGtesting.com
LVHW091147150724
785511LV00005B/589